# JOYFUL JUICING

# JOYFUL JUICING

## CAREY KINGSBURY

FRONT TABLE BOOKS

AN IMPRINT OF CEDAR FORT, INC.
SPRINGVILLE, UTAH

© 2014 Carey Kingsbury

ISBN 13: 978-1-4621-1376-7

Published by Front Table Books, an imprint of Cedar Fort, Inc.
2373 W. 700 S., Springville, UT 84663
Distributed by Cedar Fort, Inc., www.cedarfort.com

   Library of Congress Cataloging-in-Publication Data on file

Cover and page design by Erica Dixon
Cover design © 2014 by Lyle Mortimer
Edited by Casey J. Winters

Printed in the United States of America

10 9 8 7 6 5 4 3 2 1

Dedicated to Eric, Haley, and Dylan.

Written for all seekers of joy and vibrant health.

# CONTENTS

# INTRODUCTION

Juicing has made such a positive impact on my life that I want to share it with as many people as possible. There's no better method to give the body a quick and powerful burst of nutrition than fresh juice. When people ask me why I love juicing so much, I reply, "Because fruits and veggies love me back!"

I began my juicing journey on my own, with no information and no recipes. I simply knew that juicing was supposed to be good for me. When I purchased my first juice machine over thirteen years ago, I experienced a tingle of excitement. I couldn't wait to start drinking healthy and energizing juices! But then I suddenly felt a tinge of dread because I realized I had no idea how to even begin making juice. I worried that I might put the wrong foods in the juicer, and I worried that I would hate the taste of the juices and never want to make them again.

This fear continued for a few weeks while my brand-new machine sat on the counter waiting to interact with me. I couldn't handle the fact that I was serving rejection to both the juice machine and myself, so I put it away in the cabinet and closed the door.

Deep down I knew that this juice machine could help change my life for the better, but the truth is change can be difficult to process emotionally. So I played it safe for a couple of months and avoided this change altogether. But eventually my desire to be the healthy person I knew I was meant to be outweighed my desire to play it safe and stay the same forever. I brought the juice machine out of the cabinet and began experimenting with juices.

Since that day nearly thirteen years ago, I've made thousands of juices for myself, my family, and my friends. I've convinced nearly everyone I know to purchase a juicer. Each year I do at least a couple of juice cleanses (fasting with juice).

In 2008 I began a blog called MyJuice Cleanse.com so I could connect with others and share my recipes and my experiences. Though I wasn't much of a writer in the beginning, I was lucky enough to have some followers. I listened to their feedback on what they wanted to learn about, and I continued to build a useful site. Today *My Juice Cleanse* is one of the largest sources of information about juicing and cleansing on the web. There is an active and growing Facebook page (facebook.com/myjuicecleanse) and now a digital magazine called *Juice + Blend* on the iTunes app store. I am truly blessed and filled with joy every day to be a part of such a positive and healthy movement.

I want you to enjoy the process of juicing because if you do, it is likely to become a permanent part of your routine and something you can look forward to every day. To me, juicing is joy, and that's what life is all about.

## About This Book

I set out to write a book about juicing that is perhaps a bit different from others; after all, my approach to good health is a bit different from other experts. I believe that our bodies and our hearts innately have the power to guide us to make healthy choices. This inner guidance system lies outside the realm of logic and reason and nutritional facts. Instead it is connected to the Divine, and it points in the direction of joy. If we follow our inner guidance system, we can never go wrong.

Vibrant, joyful health is as much (and maybe more) about the five senses and your physical environment as it is about daily recommended allowances of vitamins. I encourage you as you read this book to take the time to explore your environment and practice the art of observation. Observe your kitchen, your foods, and your thoughts about food and health.

When you are ready to create some of the recipes in this book, notice which ones you are drawn to. Follow your inner guide and make the juices that your body and spirit wish to receive.

With love, light, and joy, I wish for you vibrant health!

# CHAPTER 1

## JOY AND VIBRANT HEALTH

### What Is Joy and Vibrant Health?

Joy and vibrant health are concepts that can seem elusive to many of us. We may know when we feel (or don't feel) joy, and we may be able to sense when we are in good health, but what are they exactly and how do we achieve them? I will share my story here in hopes that it might help you.

Nearly fourteen years ago, I began a journey to find good health and happiness. This was preceded by a period of low energy, excess weight, and depression that I couldn't seem to escape. The traditional doctors that I visited offered medication, which I reluctantly accepted, but the medication did not bring me any closer to the good health and happiness I was searching for. In fact, medication compounded the problem by causing side effects, and I soon realized that I needed to take a different approach to my healing.

I knew deep inside that there had to be a gentler way to transform my life, one that was natural and worked with my body rather than against it. Through research and experimentation, I discovered that plants and herbs used in the form of foods, juices, teas, and medicinal preparations provide the body with the nutritional compounds it needs to regenerate and heal.

My body and mind responded very well to this plant-based approach, and I began to feel energized, alive, and creative. Fresh juice became one of my favorite methods of getting nutrition into my body, and I continue making juice to this day because it literally makes me feel better within a few moments of drinking a glass. It brings me joy.

I define *joy* as a feeling of happiness accompanied by a sustained sense of well-being and harmony. In a state of joy, a high vibration of energy runs through the mind, body, and spirit. It is a palpable energy that triggers a sense of *Yes, this is right for me*! We experience joy when we are *being* and *doing* in ways that fulfill our sense of purpose in life.

The physical counterpart to joy is *vibrant health*. We naturally thrive when we are involved in activities that fulfill our body's purpose of sustaining and regenerating itself. The body responds by exhibiting energy, flexibility, and endurance, all signs of vibrant health.

## Essential Elements for Vibrant Health

Seven key elements are necessary for vibrant health. Every day we are presented with the choice whether to include these elements in our lives. The decisions we make and actions we take regarding these elements can either enhance or deplete our health. Inclusion of all these elements strengthens our well-being, whereas if we neglect any element, we risk health problems and depression.

NATURE: Sunlight, fresh air, and living plants are essential to our health. The sun is a source of energy and the basis for all life on earth. It increases the oxygen content in our blood, lowers blood pressure, and triggers our bodies to produce vitamin D for healthy bones. Fresh air is vital for living and helps us fight off disease, digest more effectively, and sleep more soundly. Plants improve the air we breathe and provide us with food, medicine, clothing, and more.

WATER: Our bodies are composed of nearly 75 percent water. We need water in every cell, tissue, and organ of the body. Water helps the body digest and absorb vitamins and minerals.

NUTRITIOUS FOOD: The foods we eat have a direct effect on our health. Nearly 68 percent of all diseases are diet related. Chronic ailments, cardiovascular disease, and degenerative illnesses can be prevented by adopting a nutritious plant-based diet.

MOVEMENT: One of the most effective ways to improve overall health is through movement and exercise. Movement can cure chronic conditions and slow the aging process. Being physically active on a regular basis contributes to improved heart-lung and muscle fitness, boosts chemicals in the brain to protect against cognitive decline, creates feelings of euphoria and happiness through the release of endorphins, increases the body's ability to relax and sleep, and protects against heart disease.

REST: Adequate downtime and sleep are important to keep the mind and body resilient. Six hours of sleep per night recharges the body's energy levels, lowers stress, reduces inflammation, improves memory, and boosts the immune system.

RELATIONSHIPS: Humans are social beings and we require interaction with others for meaning in our lives. Friendship, love, communication, and compassion all fuel our hearts and literally help us to survive. Through meditation and prayer, we communicate and create spiritual relationships with the Divine.

PASSION: Passion—or a deep desire for something—inspires action to accomplish goals. It gives meaning and structure to our lives and strengthens our confidence. Every living being is striving to be all that its nature will allow while taking into account the resources available.

To have joy and vibrant health means to live in alignment with your truth.

It means that you make decisions to be good to yourself and to enjoy yourself, no matter what is happening around you. Joy and vibrant health support you by offering confidence and freedom to express your natural gifts with the world.

Nurture joy and it grows, but deny yourself joy and the spirit wilts and feels unworthy. From a place of feeling unworthy, you will be tempted to make decisions that do not support good health, like eating unhealthy foods, avoiding exercise, and placing yourself in stressful or negative situations. These become obstacles to vibrant health.

## Obstacles to Vibrant Health

Modern society presents us with all kinds of opportunities to make decisions that are not aligned with joy or don't fulfill our purpose in life. We've been conditioned to believe that life is difficult and serious, that we must work hard first and then, if we're lucky, happiness will follow. Unfortunately, for many of us this belief leads us to overwork ourselves and make too many commitments. When stress sets in, we eat the wrong types of food and have difficulty sleeping.

This way of living is toxic because it does not elevate and honor the self, and it neglects the essential elements we need to thrive and be joyful. The result of toxic living is pain, mental stress, and myriad chronic diseases.

Chronic diseases, defined as medical conditions that are persistent and long lasting, are widespread in this culture. In 2005, 133 million Americans suffered from at least one chronic illness.[1] Each year seven out of ten deaths are attributed to chronic diseases.[2] Illnesses such as irritable bowel syndrome, fibromyalgia, arthritis, and even heart disease and cancer are all chronic diseases. We all know someone who has experienced a chronic illness. Maybe you are experiencing this now.

## Three Characteristics of Chronic Disease

1. Chronic disease does not happen overnight even though symptoms may suddenly seem to appear.

2. The symptoms of chronic disease are often vague or affect many parts of the body. Even after testing there might not be an adequate diagnosis, nor can one source for the illness be found.

3. In most cases, chronic disease is reversible with the proper lifestyle changes.

If you are reading this book and currently not able to enjoy your life to the fullest because of chronic health issues, it could be time for you to embrace change and set the course for radiant and vibrant health. Our natural state of being is balanced, happy, and glowing. We are born with bodies that are capable of boundless energy, mental clarity, and optimism.

Drinking fresh fruit and vegetable juices is a simple and healthy way to honor the body, engage with nature, and lift the spirit. Juices work with the body to cleanse away toxins and nourish the cells. Fresh juice hydrates the body, provides a boost of energy, and gives your skin a healthy glow. Many people who drink fresh juice regularly experience improvement of chronic health conditions and a return to vibrant health.

# CHAPTER 2

## THE POWER OF FRESH JUICE

### Benefits of Fresh Juice

Fresh juices extracted directly from fruits and vegetables have a powerful and positive effect on health and vitality. The body responds well to fresh juices in ways that can be observed physically and monitored scientifically. Juices rejuvenate and energize the body, they help to repair damaged cells, and they strengthen healthy cells. The alkalizing effect of juices in the body helps us resist disease, lose weight, and neutralize toxins.

### Daily Nutrition

One of the great benefits of juicing is that it helps us to reach our nutritional goals quickly. Recent USDA dietary guidelines recommend five to thirteen servings of fruits and vegetables per day, depending on your caloric intake.[1] One serving size is equal to one small apple, a half cup of raw fruits or veggies, one large orange, or one cup of leafy greens. It is difficult for many people to eat this much food each day. It's a lot of food. However, one glass of juice may contain as many nutrients as three to five or more servings of the whole food. By supplementing your diet with juices, you can obtain a powerful amount of nutrition.

### Physical Benefits

During the past decade, I have been making my own juices, researching their benefits, and listening to countless people testify about the tremendous positive impact juicing has had on their lives. Some of the easily observed benefits of juicing include increased energy, mental clarity, happier moods, improved skin tone, weight loss, and improved ability to handle stress. What's even more impressive is that many people report improvement or even complete reversal of chronic ailments and even life-threatening diseases.

A consistent routine of juicing, as well as daily inclusion of the seven essential elements for vibrant health as noted in chapter 1 may be beneficial for the following conditions:

- high blood pressure
- heart disease
- joint conditions, such as arthritis
- toxic overload
- diabetes
- digestive ailments
- depression
- allergies
- skin diseases, such as eczema and psoriasis
- fibromyalgia

## Nutrients in Fresh Juice

### Releasing Juice Nutrition from the Plant

Inside living plants are fibrous cells designed to transport nutrition throughout the plant. What we call the juice is the water and nutrients that are inside the fibers. Normally, when we chew our food, the body breaks down the fibers and releases the nutrients during the process of digestion. The process of juicing mechanically separates the juices from the fiber, and the result is a concentrated liquid nutrition.

Upon drinking, our bodies assimilate juices easily. Because they are no longer bound by fiber, the nutrients from the juice are available for immediate delivery and absorption by our cells. No other form of nutrition can impact us so quickly and efficiently.

Fresh natural juices are packed with phytonutrients that cleanse, revive, and balance our bodies. The vitamins, minerals, enzymes, chlorophyll, and amino acids readily available in juices assist the body in healing and recovering from the daily stresses it endures. When the body is recharged with these nutrients, it returns to its natural state of vibrancy and radiant, joyful health.

Every plant food has its own unique combination of nutrients. Eating a variety of fruits and vegetables and drinking their juices ensures that the body is receiving complete nutrition.

## Vitamins and Minerals

VITAMIN A: Vitamin A is a key nutrient for healthy eyes. It protects the body from bacterial and viral infections, supports the immune system, and promotes bone growth. The most common form of vitamin A found in plants is beta-carotene, a provitamin. You'll find provitamin A in sweet potatoes, carrots, butternut squash, dark leafy greens, cantaloupe, apricots, and mangos.

VITAMIN B: Eight different vitamins make up the group called the B vitamins. Each of them has their own specific purpose; however, generally the B vitamins function in cell metabolism—turning food into energy and creating new cells. The B vitamins are often found in meat sources, but some can also be found in plants such as bell peppers, spinach, potatoes, green peas, broccoli, asparagus, bananas, avocados, and dark green leafy vegetables.

VITAMIN C: Vitamin C acts as an antioxidant, protecting the cells from damage caused by free radicals. It also helps the body produce collagen, which is a protein necessary for healing wounds and retaining the elasticity of the skin. Vitamin C is most commonly known to boost the immune system and can help to protect against cardiovascular disease and reduce the risk of cancer. Foods containing vitamin C include citrus fruits, bell peppers, kiwifruits, broccoli, strawberries, cantaloupe, and tomatoes.

VITAMIN E: Vitamin E is the term for a complex of eight compounds called tocopherols and tocotrienols, which are antioxidants—they fight against the oxidation and damage of cells caused by free radicals. The body does not produce vitamin E and must therefore acquire it through the diet. It protects cell membranes, widens blood vessels (to prevent clots), and boosts the immune system. Vitamin E has been identified as beneficial for heart disease, cancer, Alzheimer's, diabetes, and liver disease. Many nuts and oils contain vitamin E as well as vegetables, including spinach, broccoli, tomatoes, and asparagus.

VITAMIN K: Coagulation of blood and wound healing is one of the primary functions of a group of compounds collectively called vitamin K. It also aids in transporting calcium to the bones and preventing the calcification of the arteries. The body is able to produce vitamin K; however, it is primarily obtained through food. Plant sources of vitamin K include spinach, kale, turnip greens, mustard greens, collard greens, brussels sprouts, broccoli, asparagus, and romaine lettuce.

MINERALS: These are the catalysts of cellular function and are essential at all levels of the body. Minerals activate enzymes and assist in nerve function, formation of bones, muscle contraction, and more. Minerals are not produced by the body and must be obtained through food, primarily plants. Lack of specific minerals can be responsible for acute and chronic health conditions. Therefore it is imperative that we consume minerals to maintain vibrant health. Some of the most essential minerals for our health include calcium, copper, iron, magnesium, phosphorous, potassium, sodium, and zinc. Eating a variety of fresh fruits and vegetables will ensure a proper balance of minerals. You can easily do this by choosing foods from each color group.

## Enzymes

Live enzymes assist the body in digesting food and utilizing nutrients. Enzymes are necessary for proper cellular function, and they are catalysts for the biochemical reactions that happen in the body. We rely on enzymes for the building and rebuilding process, and we need them for life.

Living plants contain live enzymes. When you consume raw plant foods, those enzymes work to break down the food in your stomach and allow other enzymes already present in the body to be used for other functions. However when these foods are heated, the enzymes are destroyed and not able to offer the same benefits. Juicing, then, because it does not heat fruits and vegetables, becomes the perfect way to release the enzymes so they are readily available for absorption. The only caution here is that the juice must be consumed immediately, or carefully sealed, to preserve the enzymes.

## Amino Acids

It is amazing how all the components of the body are linked together and work together to preserve and renew life. Amino acids are a perfect example of this interlinking. They are literally the building materials of which proteins are created. Different sequences of amino acids produce different types of proteins, including enzymes. In turn, these proteins contribute to the function of each cell in the body, including structural support, movement, biochemical reactions, hormonal support, transportation, and communication.

Of all the amino acids, nine of them cannot be produced by the body and must be obtained from food. These are the essential amino acids.

We rely on amino acids for vibrant health, and the absence of any one of them can result in a variety of health symptoms from exhaustion to poor digestion to a weakened immune system. Fortunately the body is resilient, so we may often reverse these symptoms by simply maintaining adequate intake of the essential amino acids.

The body does not store amino acids, so it is important to consume foods that contain amino acids on a daily basis. Fresh juices, especially those made with dark green leafy vegetables and sprouts, contain the highest concentrations of essential amino acids.

## Chlorophyll

Chlorophyll is a green pigment found in plants. Through the process of photosynthesis, chlorophyll molecules absorb sunlight and convert it into chemical energy to support growth of the plant.

The structure of chlorophyll molecules is amazingly similar to that of human red blood cells. When introduced into the body, especially in the form of juices, chlorophyll increases the red blood cell count and oxygen uptake in the blood. In turn this increases energy and also improves many blood disorders. Additionally, chlorophyll enhances the body

by improving the immune system, providing antioxidants, detoxifying cells, speeding up wound healing, and reducing body odor.

Chlorophyll is readily available in green vegetables such as lettuce, wheatgrass, spinach, kale, collards, chard, cabbage, alfalfa, watercress, parsley, celery, green peppers, broccoli, turnip greens, and sea vegetables. Green juices are wildly popular today mostly due to the super health benefits provided by the chlorophyll content of these plants.

Juices have tremendous benefits for our bodies and give us a powerful boost toward vibrant health. One glass of juice can provide a full spectrum of vitamins, minerals, and other essential nutrients. You can create unlimited combinations of juices from plant foods to provide great nutrition with delicious flavor. For starters try oranges with greens, carrots with beets, and apples with celery and cucumbers.

# CHAPTER 3

## SETTING UP A JOYFUL KITCHEN

### Juices and the Five Senses

One of the reasons juicing is so powerful is because the act of making juice is a sensual experience. It gives you an opportunity to connect to the process with all five senses. By using our sight we can choose the fruits and vegetables that look appealing to us. Nature has created these foods in a vibrant rainbow of colors, each with their own unique combination of nutrients. Orange foods, for example, contain beta-carotene, vitamin A, and vitamin C.

As fruits and vegetables pass through the juice machine, their aromas are released. The aroma of fresh produce can trigger memories in the brain and can also trigger certain physiological responses such as the activation of digestion.

Foods from nature have the most interesting textures. They can be soft, smooth, bumpy, spiky, or fuzzy. The next time you are at the grocery store, close your eyes, pick up your favorite fruit or vegetable and feel its texture. Can you tell if it is ripe just by touch? The sound your produce makes is also an indicator of its ripeness as well as the amount of water it contains. Does your produce sound crisp or juicy?

Perhaps the one sense that is stimulated the most by fresh juice is the sense of taste. Some juices are sweet, and some are tart. Still other juices are earthy or grassy or pungent or minty. It really is remarkable how many combinations of flavors can be created through juicing.

When drinking juice, you get immediate feedback from your mind, body, and spirit. It's like a rocket of pure inspiration, an invitation to the possibility of feeling better than you ever have before.

If one glass of juice offers so much to your senses and your overall health, just imagine how you could feel if you juiced several times per week. Juicing on a regular basis helps you sustain that feel-good sensation and maintain a high level of health.

Creating a habit of juicing is much easier if you dedicate a space in your kitchen for the activity. You're more likely to make juice if you see your juicer on the counter and have everything ready and available for easy use. Make your kitchen a joyful space and you will encourage healthy eating.

## A Joyful Kitchen

A joyful kitchen can be large or small, ornate or simple, but it is always a place that welcomes the creation of good food and vibrant health. A joyful kitchen provides nourishment to your entire family so they may go out into the world and be happy, successful people. A joyful kitchen is there to welcome you and your family home in the evening and support them in recharging their bodies.

Because this room is so important to your well-being, it deserves to be given some care and attention. This doesn't mean you need to spend a lot of money to upgrade or decorate—it simply means to be mindful of your intentions for the room and to create a space in which you will enjoy spending time.

Begin by observing your kitchen as it is now. How does it make you feel? Is the room bright enough? Do you feel joyful or inspired? Can you find things easily? Jot down your observations.

Next, think about the tone you intend to convey in your kitchen. You may want your kitchen to be an atmosphere of love, fun, beauty, sophistication, community, or peace. It could be modern, rustic, or trendy. What colors will reflect your intention? Write down your intentions for this space. Use these ideas when you begin to reorganize your kitchen.

Let's get your kitchen organized and ready for juicing experiences! I recommend that you take at least a day to plan and arrange your kitchen. If you're like me, your kitchen needs a good cleaning at the very least.

Have a look around and notice which areas are clean and which are cluttered. A cluttered area represents stagnant energy, perhaps around something you have not wanted to deal with or resolve. Piles of miscellaneous items and broken or unused utensils and appliances have no place in a joyful kitchen. Clean out the cluttered areas and plan a better use of the space.

The flow of your kitchen is important for efficiency and will affect your desire to use the space. Consider where you keep your utensils, glasses, and appliances. Are they within reach when you need them? Or do you have to walk across the room and back again to access your tools each time you use them? Spend some time rearranging your most important tools.

Your juice machine should have a prominent and permanent space on your countertop, especially if you intend to use it regularly. Find a location near an outlet that also has enough counter space to prep your fruits and vegetables.

You don't need to conduct a whole kitchen makeover here, but if you are aware of what appliances and utensils you intend to use on a daily basis, you can plan a workflow that makes preparing healthy foods and juices more enjoyable.

This process of reorganizing your kitchen is cleansing on many levels. It helps to align your intentions and goals with your physical reality. It also creates space, literally and energetically, for you to adopt new healthy habits.

Next, take an inventory of the foods inside your cabinet and refrigerator. Look for any expired foods and discard them. Then look for any comfort foods that you and your family eat during times of emotional stress or boredom. These may be crackers, chips, cookies, or ice cream. Consider discarding or at least limiting those foods in your home. You can replace them with nuts, seeds, and fresh or dried fruits. Most packaged foods are unhealthy and create a big distraction to living healthily, so be aware of this when you are shopping.

## Shopping for Produce and Prepping

The ideal type of produce is organic and locally grown. One of the best ways to obtain healthy organic produce is from your own garden. By growing your own foods, you satisfy the body's and soul's need to connect with nature, and if gardening is your passion, you will fulfill that need as well. However, if gardening will not work for your lifestyle, try to find a local farmers market.

Of course, supermarkets are a good option if you like convenience and a wide variety of choices. When shopping for produce, let your senses be your guide. Be open and responsive and choose fruits and vegetables that are ripe and have a vibrant color, texture, and smell. These are living foods, and the life force contained in them will nourish your body.

Wash all your produce when you get home, especially if it is not organic. This will save time when you are making juice. Berries and grapes should be thoroughly dried because any water droplets on the berries can lead to mold in the refrigerator.

# Choosing Equipment

To make fresh juice you need a juice machine. A juicer differs from a blender because it is specifically designed to separate the liquid from the fiber of fruits and vegetables. The juice contains the nutrition of the plant while the fiber has no nutritional value. While fiber is necessary for digestion and elimination, the purpose of removing the fiber in juicing is to create a concentrated supplement that is easily absorbed into your body's cells. One glass of juice may contain more nutrition than what you could consume by eating.

When purchasing a juice machine, you have many choices to consider. Ultimately the decision will come down to finding one that meets most of the needs on your checklist. Here are some factors to consider:

PRICE: When shopping for a juice machine, you will notice that the prices can range from around fifty dollars to four hundred. The price will give you some indication of quality; however, many good juicers are available at all prices. Manufacturers offer different warranties for juicers ranging from one to fifteen years.

SIZE AND DESIGN: Consider your counter space when choosing a juicer. You want to choose a model that you can keep on the counter every day. Does the size, color, and style fit your joyful kitchen?

SPEED: Each juicer operates at different speeds. This can have an effect on the quality of juice, the noise of the machine, and the time it takes for preparation and cleanup. Check the specifications to determine speed. Lower-RPM machines will create less friction, which results in a slightly higher–quality juice. The rate of speed is related to the level of noise output. Generally machines with higher speeds will produce more noise.

ASSEMBLY AND CLEANUP: Juice machines are designed to be taken apart between uses for cleaning. Some have more parts than others and require more cleanup time; however, most juicers have parts that are dishwasher safe.

FOODS YOU WILL BE JUICING: You may want to choose a juicer based on the types of foods you will be juicing. In the next couple pages I explain the four types of juicers. The first two can handle a variety of produce, and the last two are specifically designed for one type of food.

## Centrifugal Juicers

The most popular type of juicer for first-time users is the centrifugal machine. Generally these are more affordable and easier to clean. Inside the centrifugal juicer is a stainless-steel mesh basket with blades on the bottom. When you push fruits and vegetables through the chute into the machine, the blades shred them while the basket spins at high speeds. The juice is forced through the mesh sides, and the pulp either remains inside the basket or is ejected into a container on the outside.

Centrifugal juice machines can juice most any type of fruits and vegetables and are especially good with harder produce such as apples, carrots, beets, and celery, though they may not be quite as efficient with leafy greens. Don't let that deter you too much from these juicers because many are now equipped with variable speeds to accommodate both softer and harder fruits and vegetables.

In the past few years the design of the centrifugal juicers has improved. Most of these machines now have a food chute that is approximately three inches wide, enough to fit a small apple without having to cut it. This can be a time-saver and makes the act of juicing more fun and easy.

### A Note about Juice Quality of Centrifugal Juicers

The spinning process of centrifugal juicers adds oxygen, which forms as a froth on the top of the juice. Machine models with higher speeds produce more friction and often more froth. It is believed that this friction may cause some loss of nutrition in the juice. For most people this amount is not enough to cause concern, however.

## Masticating Juicers

The second category is the masticating juicer. This machine "chews" fruits and vegetables as they are pushed into the juicer and down through gears. The food is crushed and then forced through a strainer, similar to the mesh basket on the centrifugal juicer. The process generates less heat and friction than centrifugal juicers, thereby making a higher-quality, longer-lasting juice. With slower speeds, these machines take a bit longer to make juice, but they may yield more juice. The design of masticating juice machines makes them ideal for juicing green leafy vegetables, and some models will be able to juice wheatgrass. Masticating juicers are often able to grind nuts, seeds, dried fruits, and frozen bananas as well.

This type of juicer, however, is generally heavier, takes up more counter space, and is often harder to clean. Prices of masticating juicers are in the top half of the price range. Newer models created in the last couple of years are upright and easier to clean, but these are also at the very top of the price range.

## Citrus Juicers

Citrus juicers can be either manual or electric and they are made for oranges, lemons, grapefruits, and limes. If you plan to juice citrus in the mornings, this type of juicer is easy to use and easy to clean.

## Wheatgrass Juicers

Wheatgrass is the sprouted grass of the wheat berry and is highly regarded for its nutritional content and healing abilities. The wheatgrass juicer is similar to the masticating juicer in that it has a gear that slowly crushes. Most wheatgrass juicers are operated by a hand crank, which ensures a slow speed and preservation of nutrients.

## Additional Tools

Other than a juice machine, I recommend a few other small kitchen tools. You probably have many of these. If not, you can purchase them rather inexpensively.

- paring knife
- vegetable peeler
- vegetable brush
- apple corer and slicer (if your juicer won't take a whole apple)
- cutting board

# Making Your First Juice

Many people are excited about getting started juicing, and that's great. You *should* be excited! When you drink fruit or vegetable juice directly after it's been extracted, you are filling your body with the living enzymes, vitamins, and nutrients of the plants. The juices you make can have a powerful healing effect on your mind, body, and spirit. Through fresh juices, you have the potential to experience more energy, less pain, younger-looking skin, weight loss, improved mental function, prevention from diseases, and much more.

Just know that if you've never had fresh juice before, your body will appreciate a slow introduction. The first juice you make in your juice machine doesn't have to be complicated. Since most people, adults and children alike, prefer the taste of fruit juices, that is a good place to start. A simple, one-ingredient juice made from apples or oranges can delight your senses and provide vibrant nutrients to every cell in your body.

Some produce will need a little preparation before juicing. Citrus fruits should be peeled because the rind can taste bitter and, if the fruit is not organic, the rind will contain pesticide residue. The pits inside fruits like peaches, cherries, and plums should be removed before juicing. This is done for two reasons. First, the pits are simply too hard on the machine.

Second, the pits contain small amounts of cyanogenic compounds, which could be toxic in large quantities. But don't be alarmed. The body is fully capable of detoxifying small amounts of this compound. Apples and pears also contain small quantities of this compound in their seeds. Many people juice whole apples and pears daily with no consequences (myself included). However, if this is a concern for you, simply remove the core of the fruit before juicing.

I also recommend removing the green tops from carrots and beets. While some people do eat them in salads and soups, they seem to have an overpowering bitter taste for most people when juiced. This could cause symptoms of distress such as nausea, vomiting, and diarrhea. Beets in general have a very powerful detoxifying effect on the liver. Always juice beets with other vegetables and/or fruits and use sparingly.

After washing your fruits and vegetables and removing the parts that should not be juiced, cut them into pieces that will fit through your juice machine's feeding tube. The size will vary depending on your model. Follow the instructions on your machine. Lower speeds are perfect for juicing soft foods and leafy greens, while higher speeds will best handle harder foods like carrots and beets.

## Juicing with a Blender

The most ideal way to prepare your own fresh juices is with a juice machine. Blenders do not separate the juice from the fiber. Instead, they chop the fiber into a fine texture. However, sometimes you may not have a juicer available when you want to have fresh juice. A blender can make a nice substitute for a juicer, though it will take a bit of extra work on your part.

To make your juice in a blender, wash and prepare the fruits and vegetables as you normally would to make juice. Add the ingredients to the blender and blend on high until well blended.

If your mixture is too thick, add one to two cups water and blend until the mixture makes a smooth, swirling vortex.

The next step is to separate the pulp out from your blended mixture. You will need a mesh strainer or thin fabric such as cheesecloth or a nut milk bag. Place the strainer or fabric over a large pitcher or bowl and pour in the blended mixture. Let this stand until all the liquid has drained out. If you are using a fabric or nut milk bag, you can grab the edges together and squeeze with your clean hands to get the juice out faster.

## How to Store Fresh Juice

The process of extracting juice from the fibers of the fruits and vegetables releases the vital nutrients and enzymes. When the juice is exposed to air, it oxidizes or becomes less stable, and the nutrients are quickly lost. For this reason fresh juices should be consumed immediately. In some circumstances, though, you may desire to store the juice for later. This is entirely possible if you can reduce the amount of time that the juice is exposed to the air and seal it up quickly.

Juices (with a few exceptions) will keep safely in the refrigerator for up to twenty-four hours. Glass jars are best for storing juice since the plastic ones may leach chemicals. Widemouthed canning jars in either eight-ounce or sixteen-ounce sizes are ideal.

You can make a variety of juices in bulk in the morning (or the night before) and store them to share with your family or drink them during a juice cleanse. Opening the refrigerator to see a rainbow of juices is fun, and it keeps you motivated to stay healthy.

## METHOD FOR MAKING JUICES IN BULK

**YOU'LL NEED**

up to 5 recipes found in this book

juicer

up to 5 (16-oz.) canning jars

fresh produce

lemons (optional)

masking tape

permanent marker

Follow the instructions for your first recipe. Most recipes in this book make between 10 and 16 ounces of juice. You may double a recipe if desired. Fill one of the canning jars with juice. This next step is optional but may help to discourage oxidation: cut a lemon in half and squeeze 1 teaspoon of lemon juice into your jar. Seal the lid. Put a piece of masking tape on the outside and use the marker to indicate the recipe name and date/time created. Place in the refrigerator. Rinse your juicer and repeat steps for the next juices.

# Developing a Daily Routine

Nutrition is one of the seven essential elements for vibrant health. Without it, your body simply won't function at optimum levels, which can lead to frustration and depletion of joy. A daily health routine that includes juicing will help to keep your nutrition in balance so you can feel your best. You need two things to make an activity a habit that will continue for weeks, months, or even years. First, the activity must be fun and enjoyable. Second you must see a benefit in order to continue the activity. Juicing fits the bill for both of these.

There are so many ways to make the experience of juicing fun. Find some recipes in this book that you love and mark them as favorites. These will be your go-to recipes when you're tired in the morning and don't know what to make. Memorize the recipes and always have the ingredients available in your joyful kitchen.

Set aside one day per week as your fruit and vegetable shopping day. Go to the farmers market or grocery store and stock up with a basketful of colorful fresh produce. I know whenever I'm shopping, someone will always start a conversation with me about my intentions for so much produce. I happily share that I'm juicing, and it often inspires others to begin juicing too. Own it!

Personally one of the things I love most about juicing is that I can feel the benefits almost immediately. It's a subtle but powerful experience. A morning green juice gives me a feeling of stability and stimulates my brain (really!). It's my daily ritual of joy.

The best way to develop a habit of juicing is to make a juice first thing in the morning before breakfast. Juicing on an empty stomach ensures that it will be absorbed quickly into your body because it's not trying to digest other foods at the same time. Mornings are also the best time mentally to set a habit because you can get the body into motion making juice before the mind has time to object and veer you off course. After a couple of weeks of juicing once in the morning, you will most likely notice that your energy levels are consistently higher and you're not reaching for the junk foods because your body is satisfied nutritionally and your mind is inspired and focused. Once established, this routine will support your mind and body indefinitely for vibrant health and joy.

# CHAPTER 4

## JUICE CLEANSING

Sometimes, despite all your best efforts, life does go off course and you find yourself feeling less than vibrant, less than healthy. Many factors contribute to your state of health—when the balance is off, you will experience a host of symptoms and even illness.

## Toxic and Acidic Bodies

Through normal daily activities, you are exposed to numerous substances that are toxic to the body. Some of the toxins originate externally such as chemicals and pollutants found in the water, food, and air, as well as products that come into contact with the skin. Internally you also produce toxins through the normal process of metabolism.

One of the most common sources of external toxins comes from the typical modern diet of processed foods. In exchange for convenience, we can expose ourselves to products that are full of pesticides, mercury, sodium nitrate, bisphenol A (BPA), artificial sweeteners and colors, and a whole host of chemical preservatives. These chemicals do not provide nourishment. Rather, they are harmful and can cause illness if allowed to build up inside the body.

Toxins from refined foods, stress, and the environment also disrupt the pH balance within the body. Ideal pH level is slightly alkaline at 7.35; however, toxic conditions cause the pH levels to become acidic. Soda, coffee, crackers, medication, and fast food contribute to this condition, and diseases thrive in an acidic body. Signs of an acidic body include arthritis, stiff joints, itchy or dry skin, headaches, mouth ulcers, and leg spasms.

Your body does have a detoxification system to render the toxins harmless or remove them from the body. You have seven efficient pathways throughout your body to neutralize and eliminate toxins: the colon, liver, kidneys, lungs, blood, lymph, and skin. Under ideal lifestyle conditions, everything functions seamlessly and results in vibrant health. When your exposure to toxins rises, the body responds by using more energy toward detoxification.

But if the balance tips more toward the side of toxins, your body attempts to store some of those toxins in fat tissues to keep them from harming you. In turn, the body becomes overweight and tired from carrying these toxins. Accumulation of toxins interferes with normal cell functions and contributes to chronic health conditions like chronic fatigue, high blood pressure, heart disease, type 2 diabetes, and even cancer to name a few.

The body is incredible and often has the power to heal itself. Under a state of physical crisis, the body will pull its energy together in an attempt to rid itself of the source of the illness. Think about what your body does when it has a viral infection. It turns up the temperature to kill off the virus. The body may give a sign of nausea, which tells you not to eat while it detoxifies and recovers.

Throughout history, people have used fasting to assist the body in the detoxification process. Fasting allows the body to rest and gather the strength to correct imbalances. At one time water fasting would have been common, but today we have the knowledge about the benefits of adding juices to a fast. Fasting with juices is most often referred to as a juice cleanse.

## How Juice Cleansing Heals the Body

Juice cleansing is a process of consuming only juices and water (no solid food) for a short period of time, usually one to ten days. Juices alkalize, nourish, and support the body during cleansing. Juices stimulate cell regeneration and aid the body in eliminating toxins by flushing it with water and nutrients. As the toxins are flushed away, the body has no more need to hold onto fat, and you may quickly lose excess weight. The end result of a juice cleanse is a strengthening and healing of all the body systems, especially the digestive system.

As the toxins are released and the pH returns to an optimal level, the body begins to find its joy again and health conditions improve. Some of the physical benefits of juice cleansing are:

- strengthened immune system
- improved mental clarity
- weight loss
- increased energy
- less inflammation
- decreased pain
- lower blood pressure

- improved skin tone
- balanced nervous system
- elevated mood
- reduced junk food cravings

Juice cleansing transforms lives in the physical sense, but it also empowers us in mental, emotional, and spiritual ways. Cleansing allows us to disconnect from the rush of modern living. It connects us instead to the quiet voice inside that knows our purpose in life. We begin to feel a deep awareness about ourselves and the world around us. Through awareness, we can create a new discipline for how we show up in the world, how we approach the ritual of eating, and how we communicate in our relationships. With a better understanding of ourselves, we can reach out and share our gifts. This is the place where joy and peace are found.

## Getting Ready for a Cleanse

Cleansing is personal, and your reasons for conducting a cleanse will be unique to you. Do you have a "heavy" feeling? Are you "foggy headed" and mentally drained? Are you overworked and stressed out? These are all indications that your mind, body, and spirit are out of balance and could be realigned through cleansing. Trust the instincts that you get from your body and your spirit. They are communicating with you and will guide you through the process.

### Who Should Not Fast

Most people can and should do a juice fasting cleanse on a periodic basis. By doing so you assist the body in healing and balancing so that it can better support life and longevity. However, some people with certain conditions should not fast.

Juice cleansing may not be safe and is not advised for the following conditions. Consult a professional if any of these apply to you.

- extremely weakened immune system such as cancer
- diabetes
- anemia
- pregnant or nursing
- children under 18

- anorexia, bulimia, or malnutrition
- heart failure
- liver failure
- kidney failure
- tuberculosis
- low blood pressure

The body is a complex system and we are not always aware of our state of health beyond our physical symptoms. In order to maintain maximum health, you should have regular checkups with a health practitioner whom you trust and discuss any changes in your health routine with him or her. Many doctors are aware of the health benefits of juicing and can support you during the process.

## Making a Plan

Though it's tempting to jump right into your cleanse, having a plan will ensure that your results will last longer and be more meaningful. Once you've decided that a cleanse is right for you, take a moment to write down your reasons for cleansing and your goals. Envision how you will look and feel after the cleanse and write that down also. Be optimistic yet realistic and refer to your notes during your cleanse. You may get discouraged at times, and your notes will serve as motivation to stay on track.

How you prepare your body for a juice cleanse will depend on your current level of health, lifestyle, and habits. The body needs time to transition from eating mode to cleansing mode, so take it easy and be kind to yourself. I suggest you make a few dietary and lifestyle changes for the week prior to cleansing:

---

### Changes to Make Prior to a Cleanse

- Add more fruits and vegetables to your diet including raw foods, juices, and smoothies.
- Cut back or eliminate red meat and dairy.
- Hydrate by drinking more water. Drink approximately half your body weight in ounces each day (i.e., if you weigh 150 pounds, drink 75 ounces).
- Avoid soda, alcohol, coffee, refined foods, and junk foods.

---

You will probably begin to feel much better after making some of these changes. Hopefully after your cleanse you will continue to eat healthily and be kind to your body. While you're eating healthily and getting excited the week before your cleanse, you can also use this time to get some other things in order. Be prepared so you can be open and allowing of the healing process.

CLEAR YOUR SCHEDULE: Honor yourself by canceling any commitments that will be draining. Take a vacation day or two. Plan to pamper yourself during your cleanse and leave stress behind.

ORGANIZE YOUR KITCHEN: Set up your kitchen so that making juice is easy and remove any tempting junk foods. Refer to chapter 3 for more information on this.

FIND RECIPES AND MAKE A SHOPPING LIST: Look through this book and find at least five recipes to use during your cleanse. Make a shopping list for up to three days of juices. Alternatively you may choose the recipes already provided in the sample plan on page 28.

TELL YOUR FRIENDS AND FAMILY: Implementing healthy changes in your life takes courage, and telling others about your plans takes even more courage. Don't insist that anyone agree with you or join you—simply ask for understanding.

PLAN TO BEGIN your cleanse during a period of low stress or when you can be away from a heavy schedule. Weekends are a perfect time to cleanse.

## What to Expect

Everyone experiences the cleansing process differently. You may experiences some headaches in the beginning or some hunger as your body adjusts, and some aches and pains may also be present. These are all indications that toxins are being released. These physical symptoms are often referred to as a healing crisis. Rest and hydration will help you through the initial stages of the cleanse and any symptoms of a healing crisis.

One of my favorite aspects of cleansing is the experience of a heightened sense of clarity and focus. Cleansing forces us to be in the moment and feel and allow the sensations that arise. Self care, rather than the cares of the outside world, becomes the number one priority. Cleansing puts us energetically in a space to receive Divine guidance, inspiration, and joy!

## CLEANSE BOOSTERS

Toxins are neutralized or eliminated in various ways throughout the body, and you can do several activities during your juice cleanse in order to support the detoxification process and make it more effective and enjoyable. Try some of the following cleanse boosters that appeal to you.

**Light exercise and stretching** is the number one way to give your body a boost. Exercise circulates the blood and helps to oxygenate your cells, which expels toxins and gives you more energy. Walking, swimming, biking, yoga, and rebounding are good choices.

**Dry brushing** on the surface of your skin also helps to circulate the blood. Use a natural bristle brush and make short strokes along your body in the direction of your heart. Do this daily before a shower.

**Meditation** helps to quiet the mind and let go of the stresses of daily life. It has been shown to boost immunity and happiness levels. Practice meditation daily during your cleanse for maximum benefits.

**Journaling** is another way to let go of the troubles of the mind. Through journaling you may discover some thought patterns that are not serving you well, and you may choose to release them or replace them.

# THREE-DAY JUICE CLEANSE PLAN

Use this three-day plan as a guide for your cleanse or choose your own recipes from this book. Drink between twelve and sixteen ounces of juice for each meal. Try to limit your fruit juices to just one per day. Continue to hydrate with water. If you feel that you need a snack during the day, choose a water-packed food such as a peeled cucumber or peeled apple.

## Day 1

| | |
|---|---|
| Upon waking | Lemon water. Squeeze half a lemon into a glass and add 8 ounces of warm purified water. Drink immediately. |
| Breakfast | Royal Green juice (p. 67) |
| Late morning snack | Bright and Alert juice (p. 46) |
| Late morning snack | Green Turbo (p. 68) |
| Afternoon snack | Red Beet Cooler (p. 56) |
| Dinner | Royal Green juice (p. 67) |

## Day 2

| | |
|---|---|
| Upon waking | Lemon water. Squeeze half a lemon into a glass and add 8 ounces of warm purified water. Drink immediately. |
| Breakfast | Alkalizing Greens (p. 64) |
| Late morning snack | Celery Citrus juice (p. 42) |
| Late morning snack | Green Hydrating juice (p. 71) |
| Afternoon snack | Vitamin C Boost (p. 58) |
| Dinner | Green Hydrating juice (p. 71) |

## Day 3

| | |
|---|---|
| Upon waking | Lemon water. Squeeze half a lemon into a glass and add 8 ounces of warm purified water. Drink immediately. |
| Breakfast | The Chauffeur (p. 34) |
| Late morning snack | Easy Breeze (p. 45) |
| Late morning snack | Green Power juice (p. 70) |
| Afternoon snack | Green Power juice (p. 70) |
| Dinner | Joyful Heart (p. 52) |

Continue to drink purified water throughout the day. You may drink herbal tea as well. Rest as necessary and use cleanse boosters (p. 27).

## AFTER CLEANSING

On the first day following your three-day juice cleanse, consume only juices and either fruit or lightly steamed vegetables. Begin the morning with a green juice followed by a piece of fruit about fifteen minutes after that. Continue throughout the day with a juice and then either fruit or lightly steamed vegetable at each meal. Eat lightly for a few more days and continue with juices at least once per day to help the body maintain this vibrant state of health.

# CHAPTER 5

## JUICE RECIPES

I've included my best and favorite recipes here. My goal is for you to always have recipes available that taste great and help raise your level of joy and vitality. Juice daily for best results.

Each recipe will make one serving unless otherwise noted. Depending on which juice machine you use and the size and quality of your produce, you can expect to get between ten and sixteen ounces of juice per serving.

# FRUIT-BASED

SWEET BALANCE

## SWEET BALANCE

*Don't let the sweet taste of this juice fool you—it helps to regulate the digestive tract and bowels.*

1 large red plum

1 pear

1 green apple

¼-inch piece ginger

Cut produce to fit into the feeding tube of your juicer. Juice each ingredient. Pour into a glass.

## GOLDEN DELIGHT

*Yellow is synonymous with happiness and joy, so it's no wonder that this juice can help boost your mood. Beta-carotene helps to boost vision and the immune system.*

2 cups pineapple

1 yellow pepper (*Capsicum*)

1 lemon, peeled

1-inch piece ginger

Cut produce to fit into the feeding tube of your juicer. Juice each ingredient. Pour into a glass.

## SUMMER JUBILEE

*When you can find all these fruits in season, make this juice! Cherries may help reduce inflammation and lower the risk for heart disease.*

1 cup cherries

2 peaches

1 cup grapes

Remove cherry and peach pits. Cut to fit into the feeding tube of your juicer. Juice each ingredient. Pour into a glass.

## QUIET HAPPINESS

*Broccoli juice has a surprisingly sweet taste. This is a wonderful juice to drink when you want to relax for a moment.*

2 cups broccoli florets

2 pears

1 green apple

Cut produce to fit into the feeding tube of your juicer. Juice each ingredient. Pour into a glass.

## SWEET MELON

*A good choice for a warm day, this juice will quench your thirst and boost your antioxidant levels.*

¼ honeydew melon

2 cups grapes

1 cucumber

½ lime

Cut produce to fit into the feeding tube of your juicer. Juice each ingredient. Pour into a glass.

## THE CHAUFFEUR

*One of my personal favorites. So named because you can usually find me with a glass of this juice in my hand as I drive my kids to school.*

2 green apples

3 celery stalks

1 cucumber

½ lemon, peeled

½-inch piece ginger

Cut produce to fit into the feeding tube of your juicer. Juice each ingredient. Pour into a glass.

## QUIET HAPPINESS

**BERRIES 'N' BEET**

CAREY KINGSBURY

## IN THE MOMENT

*Sweet and healthy, this juice will make you forget your troubles. And you won't even taste the spinach.*

2 red apples

1 cup blueberries

1 cup spinach

Cut apples to fit into the feeding tube of your juicer. Juice each ingredient. Pour into a glass.

## BERRIES 'N' BEET

*A rich juice—deep in color, flavor, and health benefits. The ingredients in this juice help lower blood pressure and protect the heart.*

1 medium beet

1 cup blueberries

1 cup raspberries

Cut produce to fit into the feeding tube of your juicer. Juice each ingredient. Pour into a glass.

## BLUEBERRY PEAR LEMONADE

*This is my grown-up version of traditional lemonade. No sugar added, just pure fruit nutrition. Yum!*

2 anjou pears

1 large lemon, peeled

½ cup blueberries

½-inch piece ginger

Cut off pear top and skin. Cut produce to fit into the feeding tube of your juicer. Juice each ingredient. Pour into a glass.

# BEAUTY SECRET

*The secret to glowing skin is antioxidants. Kiwifruit is the secret ingredient that will give your skin a boost.*

4 carrots

2 kiwifruits

1 cucumber

½ lime, peeled

Cut produce to fit into the feeding tube of your juicer. Juice each ingredient. Pour into a glass.

# FRUIT PASSION

*Not only is this juice sweet and decadent in taste, but it also contains resveratrol and bromelain, both anti-inflammatory compounds.*

¼ of a pineapple

1 cup strawberries

1 cup black grapes

1 pear

Cut off pineapple top and skin. Cut produce to fit into the feeding tube of your juicer. Juice each ingredient. Pour into a glass.

# GREEN GODDESS

*Exotic, green, and full of flavor, this juice offers cardio-vascular and lung support.*

2 kiwifruits

1 pear

½ lime

2 kale leaves

Cut produce to fit into the feeding tube of your juicer. Juice each ingredient. Pour into a glass.

## GREEN GODDESS

# CITRUS ENERGY

CAREY KINGSBURY

## CITRUS ENERGY

1 orange, peeled

1 lemon, peeled

¼ grapefruit, peeled

¼ cucumber

½-inch piece ginger

Segment citrus fruit. Cut cucumber and ginger to fit into the feeding tube of your juicer. Juice each ingredient. Pour into a glass. This juice serves 2.

## BRIGHT SKIN

1 carrot

1 green apple

1 cup cantaloupe

1 orange, peeled

Cut produce to fit into the feeding tube of your juicer. Juice each ingredient. Pour into a glass.

## LUSCIOUS BLACKBERRY

*Blackberries are at the top of the charts in terms of anti-oxidant content. They're beneficial for cardiovascular, skin, and eye health as well as cancer prevention.*

2 cups blackberries

1 red apple

1 pear

¼-inch piece ginger root

¼ lemon, peeled

Cut produce to fit into the feeding tube of your juicer. Juice each ingredient. Pour into a glass.

# PURE BLISS

*Your kids won't even know this juice contains carrots, but they may ask for more.*

3 carrots

2 red apples

1 cup strawberries

½-inch slice ginger

Cut produce to fit into the feeding tube of your juicer. Juice each ingredient. Pour into a glass.

# ORCHARD TWIST

*Basil is a fragrant spice that offers a spicy flavor to this otherwise sweet juice. It contains antibacterial properties and cardiovascular benefits. A little bit goes a long way, so all you need are a few leaves.*

2 apples

2 pears

1 mango, peeled and pitted

1 cup strawberries

4 basil leaves

Cut produce to fit into the feeding tube of your juicer. Juice each ingredient. Pour into a glass.

# CELERY CITRUS

*I'm not a big celery fan, but I discovered this combination and it changed my opinion.*

4 celery stalks

2 red apples

8–10 strawberries

2 oranges, peeled

Cut produce to fit into the feeding tube of your juicer. Juice each ingredient. Pour into a glass.

## CELERY CITRUS

## RADIANCE

CAREY KINGSBURY

# EASY BREEZE

*Packed with enzymes and vitamin C, this juice has become a favorite among almost everyone who tries it.*

½ orange, peeled

1 lemon, peeled

2 cups pineapple

1–2 mint sprigs

Segment the citrus fruits to fit into the feeding tube of your juicer. Juice each ingredient. Pour into a glass.

# SUNNY MORNING

*Hydration, energy, and endurance are the powerful benefits of this juice combo. It helps me get through an entire morning with ease.*

2 oranges

2 lemons

½ grapefruit

Peel citrus. Segment fruit to fit into the feeding tube of your juicer. Juice each ingredient. Pour into a glass.

# RADIANCE

1 apple

1 orange, peeled

4 carrots

¼-inch piece ginger root

Cut produce to fit into the feeding tube of your juicer. Juice each ingredient. Pour into a glass.

# VERY BERRY

*Red and purple berries contain antiaging properties as well as benefits for the heart.*

1 cup red grapes

5 strawberries

¾ cup pineapples

¼ cup raspberries

¼ cup blueberries

Cut produce to fit into the feeding tube of your juicer. Juice each ingredient. Pour into a glass.

# STRAWBERRY COCONUT COCKTAIL

*Coconut water is an excellent source of electrolytes that helps to keep you hydrated during periods of exercise or other loss of fluids. This tropical juice is a great choice for a hot summer day.*

15 strawberries

1 pear

½ lime, peeled

¾ cup coconut water

Cut produce to fit into the feeding tube of your juicer. Juice each ingredient except coconut water. Pour juice into a glass. Stir coconut water into juice.

# BRIGHT AND ALERT

*Pineapple is detoxifying to the body and, along with carrots and apples, boosts the immune system.*

½ pineapple

1 carrot

1 apple

1 celery stalk

Cut off pineapple top and skin. Cut produce to fit into the feeding tube of your juicer. Juice each ingredient. Pour into a glass.

## STRAWBERRY COCONUT COCKTAIL

## CANTALOUPE FRESCA

CAREY KINGSBURY

FRUIT-BASED

# ORANGE DREAM

*This juice is simply pure happiness for me. One sip and I melt into a relaxed, dreamy state.*

2 oranges, peeled

¼ pineapple

4 oz. coconut water

Cut produce to fit into the feeding tube of your juicer. Juice each ingredient except coconut water. Pour juice into a glass. Stir coconut water into juice.

# SWEET MELON

*A good choice for a warm day, this juice will quench your thirst and boost your antioxidant levels.*

¼ honeydew melon

2 cups grapes

1 cucumber

½ lime

Cut produce to fit into the feeding tube of your juicer. Juice each ingredient. Pour into a glass.

# CANTALOUPE FRESCA

*Cantaloupe contains large amounts of vitamin A for healthy skin and eyes. The sparkling mineral water and mint brighten up the sweetness of the cantaloupe in this refreshing drink.*

3 cups cantaloupe (½ melon)

1 mint sprig

8 oz. sparkling mineral water

Cut produce to fit into the feeding tube of your juicer. Juice each ingredient except mineral water. Pour juice into a glass. Stir mineral water into juice.

# VEGETABLE-BASED

## JOYFUL HEART

*This super healthy and delicious combo will make your heart sing physically and spiritually.*

2 carrots

1 cucumber

1 beet

1 lemon, peeled

½ cup spinach, packed

Cut produce to fit into the feeding tube of your juicer. Juice each ingredient. Pour into a glass.

## HEALTH PROTECTOR

*Cabbage is a great health protector that is often over-looked. It helps to lower cholesterol, supports the respiratory tract, and is a great anti-inflammatory agent.*

2 apples

2 carrots

1 green cabbage wedge

1 red cabbage wedge

Cut produce to fit into the feeding tube of your juicer. Juice each ingredient. Pour into a glass.

## TOMATO PEP

*Give your heart a boost with this delicious and spicy blend. Tomatoes and bell peppers have antioxidant properties, watercress and parsley are natural blood purifiers, and garlic helps to lower cholesterol.*

3 large tomatoes

1 small handful watercress

1 bell pepper

1 clove garlic

1 small handful parsley

Cut produce to fit into the feeding tube of your juicer. Juice each ingredient. Pour into a glass.

## BRAINS AND BRAWN

*Beets are brain food and spinach is muscle food. Combine them together for a powerful health drink!*

2 beets

3 celery stalks

1 pear

1 carrot

1 cup spinach

Cut produce to fit into the feeding tube of your juicer. Juice each ingredient. Pour into a glass.

## JOYFUL HEART

**MELLOW CELERY**

CAREY KINGSBURY

# JUICY RED KICKER

*Kick it up a notch with this south-of-the-border-styled juice. Using these ingredients will stimulate your immune system and make you glad you did.*

1 cup grape tomatoes

1 cucumber

1 red bell pepper

5 basil leaves

pinch salt

pinch cayenne pepper

Cut produce to fit into the feeding tube of your juicer. Juice each ingredient except salt and cayenne pepper. Pour juice into a glass. Stir in salt and cayenne pepper.

# DELIGHTFUL GREEN

*Earthy and sweet, this juice supports a healthy digestive tract.*

1 apple

½ cucumber

¼ green cabbage

1 cup spinach

Cut produce to fit into the feeding tube of your juicer. Juice each ingredient. Pour into a glass.

# MELLOW CELERY

*No joke, this juice really does mellow your mood and calm your nerves.*

4 celery stalks

2 cups broccoli florets

½ cucumber

½ lemon

Cut produce to fit into the feeding tube of your juicer. Juice each ingredient. Pour into a glass.

## SALAD IN A GLASS

*Yes, if you put your salad into a juice machine, it really would be a salad in a glass—and it would taste absolutely wonderful.*

3 carrots

2 green onions

½ bell pepper

6 romaine lettuce leaves

2 medium tomatoes

¼ cup parsley

½ lemon, peeled

Cut produce to fit into the feeding tube of your juicer. Juice each ingredient. Pour into a glass.

## VEGETABLE-8

*You know of the popular bottled drink with a similar name. Now you can make your own healthy version anytime you want.*

2 medium tomatoes

1 cucumber

2 carrots

2 celery stalks

1 cup spinach

¼ head cabbage

½ red bell pepper

1 green onion

Cut produce to fit into the feeding tube of your juicer. Juice each ingredient. Pour into a glass.

## SOUTHERN BOUNTY

*I love the flavor when tomatoes and greens are mixed together. It's tart and earthy and reminds me of the family garden. Add a little garlic spice for some heart protection and it's complete.*

¼ lemon

1 garlic clove

6 romaine lettuce leaves

3 tomatoes

½ cucumber

Cut produce to fit into the feeding tube of your juicer. Juice each ingredient. Pour into a glass.

## RED BEET COOLER

*Beets are powerful detoxifiers. They stimulate the liver and the lymphatic system to keep the body healthy.*

1 small or medium beet

4 carrots

2 oranges, peeled

8–10 mint leaves

Cut produce to fit into the feeding tube of your juicer. Juice each ingredient. Pour into a glass.

## POST-HOLIDAY JUICE

*I created this juice post–Christmas holiday dinner when I was feeling full and lethargic. It works quite well to energize the cells and clear out that heavy feeling.*

1 carrot

½ red bell pepper

1 small beet

1 apple

2 celery stalks

1 orange, peeled

½ lemon, peeled

¼ tsp. turmeric powder

Cut produce to fit into the feeding tube of your juicer. Juice each ingredient except turmeric powder. Pour juice into a glass. Stir in turmeric powder.

## CARROT BEET BLEND

4 carrots

½ beet

2 celery stalks

3 broccoli florets

Cut produce to fit into the feeding tube of your juicer. Juice each ingredient. Pour into a glass.

## DEEP-ROOTED LOVE

*Root vegetables absorb the highest amount of minerals from the soil, and we need them for proper cell functioning. The rich taste of beets and carrots is lightened and brightened by the orange and purified water.*

1 large beet

4 medium carrots

1 orange, peeled

4 oz. purified water

Cut produce to fit into the feeding tube of your juicer. Juice each ingredient except water. Pour juice into a glass. Stir in purified water.

## HEAD-TO-HEART TONIC

*The vegetables in this blend support everything from your head to your heart. Antioxidants protect against free radical damage that causes premature aging. The nutrients of vitamin A and lutein support eye health, while lycopene protects against heart disease.*

2 kale leaves

1 red bell pepper

2 carrots

½ lemon

⅛ cup parsley

7 grape tomatoes

Cut produce to fit into the feeding tube of your juicer. Juice each ingredient. Pour into a glass.

## VITAMIN C BOOST

2 oranges, peeled

3 carrots

1 lemon

½ red bell pepper

1-inch piece ginger

Cut produce to fit into the feeding tube of your juicer. Juice each ingredient. Pour into a glass.

## TOMATO JAZZ

1 beet

2 tomatoes

5 large spinach leaves

2 carrots

½ lime, peeled

pinch salt

dash pepper

Cut produce to fit into the feeding tube of your juicer. Juice each ingredient except salt and pepper. Pour juice into a glass. Stir salt and pepper into juice.

## STALKS AND SPEARS

5 asparagus spears

4 carrots

2 celery stalks

Cut produce to fit into the feeding tube of your juicer. Juice each ingredient. Pour into a glass.

## HEAD-TO-HEART TONIC

## SWEET EARTH

CAREY KINGSBURY

## SWEET EARTH

*The taste of this juice is very creamy and delightful. Sweet potatoes contain vitamins B6, C, and D as well as iron and magnesium. They benefit the heart, blood, and immune system.*

1 medium sweet potato

1 green apple

2 carrots

1-inch slice ginger root

Cut produce to fit into the feeding tube of your juicer. Juice each ingredient. Pour into a glass.

## POTASSIUM-RICH GREEN JUICE

1 celery stalk

4 medium carrots

1 cup spinach leaves

¼ cup parsley

½ lemon, peeled

Cut produce to fit into the feeding tube of your juicer. Juice each ingredient. Pour into a glass.

## YELLOW VIBE

*Simple, delicate, and crisp are three words I use to describe the Yellow Vibe juice.*

1 cucumber

1 yellow bell pepper

¼ lemon, peeled

Cut produce to fit into the feeding tube of your juicer. Juice each ingredient. Pour into a glass.

# GREEN

## GRAPES AND GREENS

1½ cucumbers

1 cup green grapes

3 large swiss chard leaves

3 large romaine lettuce leaves

Cut cucumber to fit into the feeding tube of your juicer. Juice each ingredient. Pour into a glass.

## BLUE-GREEN LEMONADE

*In this green juice, the greens step back and let the fruits take center stage. The flavor is lighter than regular green juice and just a bit tart with the extra lemon.*

3 kale leaves

1 cucumber

2 pears

½ cup blueberries

1 lemon, peeled

Cut produce to fit into the feeding tube of your juicer. Juice each ingredient. Pour into a glass.

## ALKALIZING GREENS

*Greens have an alkalizing effect on the body, which helps to keep the immune system strong.*

2 handfuls spinach

1 cucumber

3 broccoli florets (about 1 cup)

2 kale leaves

1 lemon, peeled

1 green apple (optional)

Cut produce to fit into the feeding tube of your juicer. Juice each ingredient. Pour into a glass.

## BETA-CAROTENE GREENS

4 swiss chard leaves

4 kale leaves

4 carrots

1 green bell pepper

1 lemon, peeled

Cut produce to fit into the feeding tube of your juicer. Juice each ingredient. Pour into a glass.

**GRAPES AND GREENS**

**ROYAL GREEN**

CAREY KINGSBURY

## ROYAL GREEN

*I imagine if the Royal Family ever had green juice it would be similar to this one. The flavors are subtle and sophisticated while still being powerful and commanding respect.*

1 pear

1 cucumber

½-inch slice ginger

3 cups baby spinach

½ lemon, peeled

Cut produce to fit into the feeding tube of your juicer. Juice each ingredient. Pour into a glass.

## VEGGIES 'N' SPROUTS

4 celery stalks

1 cucumber

2 handfuls spinach

8 lettuce leaves

½ cup packed alfalfa sprouts

Cut produce to fit into the feeding tube of your juicer. Juice each ingredient. Pour into a glass.

## MELON GREEN

2 red apples

1 cup cantaloupe

3 kale leaves

2 swiss chard leaves

Cut produce to fit into the feeding tube of your juicer. Juice each ingredient. Pour into a glass.

# MEAN GREEN

*This is a version of the classic Mean Green Juice made popular by Joe Cross. I like to add spinach for a slightly more mellow flavor—and also because spinach is my favorite green food.*

3 kale leaves

1 cup spinach

1 cucumber

4 celery stalks

½ lemon

½-inch piece ginger

Cut produce to fit into the feeding tube of your juicer. Juice each ingredient. Pour into a glass.

# GREEN TURBO

*This is my classic go-to green juice. When I drink it, I can actually feel the nutrients enter my system and fill my body with substance and energy. The parsley assists in detoxification as well.*

½ cup packed spinach

3 kale leaves

2 green apples

2 celery stalks

½ cup parsley

1 cucumber

½ lemon, peeled

½-inch piece ginger

Cut produce to fit into the feeding tube of your juicer. Juice each ingredient. Pour into a glass.

# INNER BALANCE

*The flavor of the Inner Balance juice is delicate and understated, and it makes me feel connected to the Divine.*

1 small zucchini

1 cup broccoli florets

½ cucumber

1 cup baby spinach

1 orange, peeled

Cut produce to fit into the feeding tube of your juicer. Juice each ingredient. Pour into a glass.

GREEN TURBO

## ANTI-INFLAMMATORY CINNAMON

*Powdered herbs can be stirred into juices for extra flavor and health benefits. Cinnamon has strong anti-inflammatory properties.*

4 large carrots

2 celery stalks

1 apple

½ cup spinach

¼ tsp. cinnamon

Cut produce to fit into the feeding tube of your juicer. Juice each ingredient except cinnamon. Pour juice into a glass. Stir in cinnamon.

## GREEN POWER

*Kale is one of the most popular greens because of its high nutrient content. It is full of vitamins A, C, and K as well as calcium and iron.*

1 green apple

2 handfuls spinach

6 kale leaves

3 carrots

½-inch piece ginger root

Cut produce to fit into the feeding tube of your juicer. Juice each ingredient. Pour into a glass.

# GREENS 'N' GARLIC

1½ cucumbers

2 handfuls spinach

½ cup cabbage

3 carrots

1 garlic

½ lemon, peeled

Cut produce to fit into the feeding tube of your juicer. Juice each ingredient. Pour into a glass.

# DOWN TO EARTH

½ cup chopped cabbage

3 celery stalks

1 cucumber

1 cup packed spinach leaves

2 apples

Cut produce to fit into the feeding tube of your juicer. Juice each ingredient. Pour into a glass.

# GREEN HYDRATING

*Apples and cucumbers are bursting with juice. Add a couple of greens like spinach and celery and you have a hydrating glass of green nutrition.*

4 ribs of celery

1 cucumber

1 green apple

1 cup spinach

½ lemon, peeled

Cut produce to fit into the feeding tube of your juicer. Juice each ingredient. Pour into a glass.

# WHEATGRASS SUPREME

CAREY KINGSBURY

# WHEATGRASS SUPREME

*For some people, the taste of wheatgrass is just too strong, but I quite like it. This young grass has some of the highest nutritional properties of all the greens, and natural health practitioners often recommend its juice for cancer prevention and treatment.*

1 green apple

1 orange, peeled

2 fistfuls spinach

1 fistful wheatgrass

½ cucumber

Cut produce to fit into the feeding tube of your juicer. Juice each ingredient. Pour into a glass.

# ARUGULA GREEN JUICE

1 romaine lettuce heart

½ cup arugula

2 pears

½ lemon, peeled

Cut produce to fit into the feeding tube of your juicer. Juice each ingredient. Pour into a glass.

# HONEYDEW GREEN TONIC

4 kale leaves

1 cup green honeydew melon

1 large cucumber

¼ cup parsley

Cut produce to fit into the feeding tube of your juicer. Juice each ingredient. Pour into a glass.

# DETOXIFYING

## BLACKBERRY DETOX

½ large beet

2 plums, pits removed

1 cup blackberries

½-inch piece ginger

Cut produce to fit into the feeding tube of your juicer. Juice each ingredient. Pour into a glass.

## APPLE BEET DETOX

1 apple

1 beet

1 orange

¾ lemon

handful parsley

Cut produce to fit into the feeding tube of your juicer. Juice each ingredient. Pour into a glass.

## DETOX TRIO

*Sometimes simple juices are best. This juice has only three ingredients, but they each have impressive cleansing abilities.*

2 green apples

2 carrots

2 celery ribs

Cut produce to fit into the feeding tube of your juicer. Juice each ingredient. Pour into a glass.

## BLACKBERRY DETOX

## SINUS RESCUE

2 tomatoes

½ cucumber

5 radishes

¼ lemon, peeled

Cut produce to fit into the feeding tube of your juicer. Juice each ingredient. Pour into a glass.

## SEE CLEARLY NOW

*Watercress and carrots both contain nutrients that are beneficial to eye health.*

1 small handful watercress (¼ cup)

1 apple

2 carrots

½ lemon, peeled

Cut produce to fit into the feeding tube of your juicer. Juice each ingredient. Pour into a glass.

## TURMERIC DETOX

1 romaine lettuce heart

2-inch turmeric root

2 carrots

1 cucumber

½ lemon, peeled

Cut produce to fit into the feeding tube of your juicer. Juice each ingredient. Pour into a glass.

## DANDELION DETOX

*Dandelion greens can be purchased at your local grocery store, but you might already have them in your backyard. The leaves are considered a dark leafy green and have many of the same properties as other leafy greens. Dandelion is especially important for liver detoxification.*

½ cup (handful) dandelion greens

4 carrots

1 cucumber

1 lemon, peeled

Cut produce to fit into the feeding tube of your juicer. Juice each ingredient. Pour into a glass.

# JOYFUL DETOX

*There comes a point in any juice cleanse, usually around the third day, when the body and mind finally begin to feel lighter and joyful. Every time I drink this juice I know I am one step closer to joy!*

1 cucumber

½ beet

3 chard leaves

2 celery stalks

1 small handful cilantro

½ lemon, peeled

½-inch piece ginger

Cut produce to fit into the feeding tube of your juicer. Juice each ingredient. Pour into a glass.

# CLEANSING JUICE

3 carrots

½ beet root

1 cucumber

⅛ cup parsley

Cut produce to fit into the feeding tube of your juicer. Juice each ingredient. Pour into a glass.

# ZEST FOR LIFE

*Due to its peppery taste and powerful detoxification properties, parsley is best used in small amounts. This herb binds with heavy metals so they may be flushed from the body.*

6 carrots

⅛ cup parsley leaves

1 clove garlic

Cut produce to fit into the feeding tube of your juicer. Juice each ingredient. Pour into a glass.

# CLEANSE ASSIST

2 cups kale

½ cup dandelion greens

1 pear

¼ lemon, peeled

Cut produce to fit into the feeding tube of your juicer. Juice each ingredient. Pour into a glass.

CAREY KINGSBURY

# DIGESTIVE CARE

## ULCER CARE

CAREY KINGSBURY

## DIGEST EASE

½ cucumber

1 green apple

1 fennel stalk with leaves

2 mint sprigs

¼- to ½-inch piece of ginger

Cut produce to fit into the feeding tube of your juicer. Juice each ingredient. Pour into a glass.

## ULCER CARE

*In studies involving 92 patients with ulcers, 95.9 percent of the patients were pain free within two weeks after drinking cabbage juice daily.*[1]

2 cups green cabbage

2 cups spinach

3 green chard leaves

3 celery stalks

1 green apple

Cut produce to fit into the feeding tube of your juicer. Juice each ingredient. Pour into a glass.

## KEEP THE DOCTOR AWAY

3 large swiss chard leaves

1 cup chopped red cabbage

2 carrots

1 red apple

¼-inch piece ginger

Cut produce to fit into the feeding tube of your juicer. Juice each ingredient. Pour into a glass.

## DIGESTIVE HARMONY

2 celery stalks

1 apple

½ fennel bulb

½ cucumber

Cut produce to fit into the feeding tube of your juicer. Juice each ingredient. Pour into a glass.

## BLISSFUL MOMENT

*The herb fennel has a mild licorice flavor and is known to ease the stomach and the mood. All the ingredients in this juice help the body to relax and de-stress.*

2 fennel stalks with leaves

2 celery stalks

3 carrots

1 pear

½-inch piece ginger

Cut produce to fit into the feeding tube of your juicer. Juice each ingredient. Pour into a glass.

# WEIGHT-LOSS

## GRAPEFRUIT CARROT ZINGER

2 grapefruits, peeled

5 carrots

½-inch piece ginger

Cut produce to fit into the feeding tube of your juicer. Juice each ingredient. Pour into a glass.

## PINEAPPLE CLEANSING JUICE

¼ pineapple

1 apple

½ beet root

2 carrots

¼ cup parsley

¼-inch piece ginger root

Cut produce to fit into the feeding tube of your juicer. Juice each ingredient. Pour into a glass.

## PINEAPPLE JOY

*Pineapple contains essential vitamins, minerals, and enzymes that assist the body in digestion, detoxification, energy, and cell renewal. These are necessary for maintaining healthy weight.*

2½ cups pineapple

1 green apple

1 lemon, peeled

10 mint leaves

Cut produce to fit into the feeding tube of your juicer. Juice each ingredient. Pour into a glass.

## GRAPEFRUIT CARROT ZINGER

## EASY BREEZY
## CUCUMBER COOLER

4 carrots

1 cucumber

1 celery stalk

1 apple

½ lemon, peeled

Cut produce to fit into the feeding tube of your juicer. Juice each ingredient. Pour into a glass.

## BEET GRAPEFRUIT

1 apple

½ grapefruit, peeled

½ cup green grapes

¼ lemon, peeled

½ small beet

Cut produce to fit into the feeding tube of your juicer. Juice each ingredient. Pour into a glass.

## SLIM DOWN

*All juices help the body to slim down; however, the fruits and vegetables in this juice help the body release extra water weight and toxins that bind to fat.*

5 carrots

1 apple

½ cucumber

½ beet

1–2 celery stalks

Cut produce to fit into the feeding tube of your juicer. Juice each ingredient. Pour into a glass.

## WATERMELON
## WEIGHT LOSS

1 cup watermelon cubes

1 cup chopped kale

1 small artichoke

3 carrots

½ lemon, peeled

Cut produce to fit into the feeding tube of your juicer. Juice each ingredient. Pour into a glass.

# NOTES

## Chapter 1

1. Shin-Yi Wu and Anthony Green, *Projection of Chronic Illness Prevalence and Cost Inflation*, Santa Monica, CA: RAND Health, 2000. From "Chronic Diseases and Health Promotion," Centers for Disease Control and Prevention, last modified August 13, 2012, http://www.cdc.gov/chronicdisease/overview/index.htm.

2. Hsiang-Ching Kung, Donna L. Hoyert, Jiaquan Xu, and Sherry L. Murphy, "Deaths: Final Data for 2005," *National Vital Statistics Reports* 56, no. 10 (April 2008), http://www.cdc.gov/nchs/data/nvsr/nvsr56/nvsr56_10.pdf.

## Chapter 2

1. US Department of Agriculture and US Department of Health and Human Services, *Dietary Guidelines for Americans, 2010*, 7th ed. (Washington, DC: US Government Printing Office, 2010).

## Chapter 5

1. Garnett Cheney, "Vitamin U Therapy of Peptic Ulcer," *California Medicine* 77, no. 4 (October 1952): 248–52, https://www.seleneriverpress.com/images/pdfs/VITAMIN_U_THERPAY_OF_PEPTIC_ULCER_by_G_CHENEY_1952_REPRINT_91.pdf.

# INDEX

# ABOUT THE AUTHOR

**C**AREY KINGSBURY knew she was born to guide and inspire others. Her mission has been to discover the energy that flows through all things and all the ways to channel that energy into positive personal outcomes. While Carey enjoyed a career as an accomplished artist, in 2008 she began to write and blog about joyful living through good health. She launched the popular blog *My Juice Cleanse* and has since become a leading authority in juicing. Through her blog and through personalized mentoring, she has helped countless people discover their own greatness and joy.